W9-ALL-912

WORLD BOOK'S
LIBRARY OF NATURAL DISASTERS

BLIZZARDS

WORLD
BOOK

a Scott Fetzer company
Chicago
www.worldbookonline.com

World Book, Inc.
233 N. Michigan Avenue
Chicago, IL 60601
U.S.A.

For information about other World Book publications, visit our Web site at
http://www.worldbookonline.com or call **1-800-WORLDBK (967-5325)**.

For information about sales to schools and libraries, call **1-800-975-3250 (United States)**;
1-800-837-5365 (Canada).

2008 revised printing

Library of Congress Cataloging-in-Publication Data

Blizzards.
        p. cm. -- (World Book's library of natural disasters)
    Summary: "A discussion of a major type of natural
disaster, including descriptions of some of the most
destructive; explanations of these phenomena, what
causes them, and where they occur; and information
about how to prepare for and survive these forces of
nature. Features include an activity, glossary, list of
resources, and index"--Provided by publisher.
    Includes bibliographical references and index.
    ISBN 978-0-7166-9802-9
    1. Blizzards--Juvenile literature.
I. World Book, Inc.
QC926.32.B65 2007
363.34'925--dc22
                        2007008816

World Book's Library of Natural Disasters
Set ISBN: 978-0-7166-9801-2

Printed in China
2 3 4 5 6 12 11 10 09 08

Editor in Chief: Paul A. Kobasa

Supplementary Publications
    Associate Director: Scott Thomas
    Managing Editor: Barbara A. Mayes

Editors: Jeff De La Rosa, Nicholas Kilzer,
    Christine Sullivan, Kristina A. Vaicikonis,
    Marty Zwikel

Researchers: Cheryl Graham, Jacqueline Jasek

Manager, Editorial Operations
    (Rights & Permissions): Loranne K. Shields

Graphics and Design
    Associate Director: Sandra M. Dyrlund
    Associate Manager, Design: Brenda B. Tropinski
    Associate Manager, Photography: Tom Evans
    Designer: Matt Carrington

Product development: Arcturus Publishing Limited
Writer: Philip Steele
Editors: Nicola Barber, Alex Woolf
Designer: Jane Hawkins
Illustrator: Stefan Chabluk

Acknowledgments:

AP Photo: 31 (Curtis Compton), 33 (Associated Press), 34 (Chris Gardner).

The Art Archive: 18 (Musée de L'Armée Paris/ Dagli Orti).

Chicago History Museum: 20 (DN-0061476/ courtesy of the Chicago Daily News collection), 38 (ICHi-37485).

Corbis: cover/ title page (Grafton Marshall Smith/ Jose Luis Pelaez), 4 (Ramin Talaie), 5 (Galen Rowell), 7 (Daniel J. Cox),
    9, 12, 13, 19, 26, 27, 28, 32, 39 (Bettmann), 14, 22, 23 (Reuters), 16 (Andrea Merola/ epa), 17 (Everett Kennedy Brown/
    epa), 29 (Frank Leonhardt/ epa), 30, 41 (Michael S. Yamashita), 36 (Colin McPherson), 40 (Philippe Eranian).

Getty Images: 35 (Tom Mihalek/ AFP).

NASA: 8 (MODIS Rapid Response Team at NASA GSFC).

National Oceanic and Atmospheric Administration/Department of Commerce: 37 (American Red Cross).

Nebraska State Historical Society Photograph Collections: 10, 11.

New Hampshire State Library: 6.

Science Photo Library: 15 (Claus Lunau/ Bonnier Publications), 24 (W. Bacon), 42 (Dr. Juerg Alean), 43 (David Hay Jones).

Thunder Bay Sanctuary Research Collection, Alpena, Michigan: 21 (Labadie Collection).

University of Washington Libraries, Special Collections: 25 (A. Curtis 17463).

TABLE OF CONTENTS

Glossary There is a glossary of terms on pages 45-46. Terms defined in the glossary are in type **that looks like this** on their first appearance on any spread (two facing pages).

Additional resources Books for further reading and recommended Web sites are listed on page 47. Because of the nature of the Internet, some Web site addresses may have changed since publication. The publisher has no responsibility for any such changes or for the content of cited sources.

WHAT IS A BLIZZARD?

A blizzard is a heavy, blinding snowstorm driven by high winds. The winds may blow the snow as it is falling, or they may whip up snow from the ground to create what is sometimes referred to as a **ground blizzard.** Both effects may occur at the same time. In the United States, the National Weather Service describes a blizzard as large amounts of falling or blowing snow with winds that blow at least 35 miles (56 kilometers) per hour for more than three hours. Blizzard conditions exist when the snow reduces **visibility** to ¼ mile (400 meters) or less.

Where do blizzards occur?

Blizzards can occur in any part of the world that experiences cold conditions. They are common in the **Arctic** and nearby regions. They are also common in coastal areas of **Antarctica.** Although southern **polar** regions get less snow than the Arctic, fierce Antarctic winds can whip up snow on the ground to create a blizzard.

A man shovels snow from sidewalks in New York City's Times Square after a February 2006 blizzard dumped more than 1 foot (30 centimeters) of snow on the city overnight.

Blizzards occur in many mountainous or **plateau** regions, including the mountain chains of the northwestern coast of North America, the southern Andes Mountains in Chile, or the plateau of Tibet in eastern Asia. These places experience cold temperatures and severe winds because of their high **altitude** rather than their closeness to Earth's polar regions.

Extreme blizzards may occur seasonally in regions where cold polar **air currents** run into milder air currents with more moisture. These are ideal conditions for creating heavy snowfalls. Such areas include many populated regions of the **Northern Hemisphere,** including southern Canada and the northern United States, where the **Great Plains** and areas around the Great Lakes can receive extreme snowfalls in winter. Blizzards may also strike Scandinavia and northern and eastern Europe, Russia, and the far north of China, Japan, and the Korean Peninsula.

Danger zones

Blizzards in remote polar or mountainous regions may pose dangers for small isolated communities or for hunters, hikers, and climbers. However, in areas with larger populations, blizzards can become full-scale natural disasters. When blizzards strike towns or cities, they can cause accidents, injuries, and deaths, as well as serious damage to property and the economy.

A climber ascends the west ridge of Mount Everest in blizzard conditions. Extreme cold, high winds, and lack of visibility during blizzards are all great dangers for mountaineers and climbers.

Before weather science

In ancient and medieval times, farmers and townsfolk usually knew which **prevailing winds** brought heavy snows. They also would have recognized other signs of an approaching storm—for example, that the wide, towering banks of clouds, which scientists today call nimbostratus, often bring heavy rain or snow. People also relied on sayings passed down from one generation to the next to predict the weather, such as "A halo around the moon, rain or snow will follow soon." In addition, people closely observed animal behavior to predict the weather. For instance, birds may fly low or roost (settle into trees) before a storm. In some cultures, dreams or visions offer weather forecasts. Among the Inuit people of the **Arctic,** a dream of birds was interpreted as a blizzard was on the way.

The Great Snow of 1717

"As mighty a snow as perhaps has been known in the memory of man," is how the Puritan minister Cotton Mather described a blizzard that is still known as the "Great Snow" of 1717. The blizzard, which pummeled southern New England, was actually a series of four snowstorms that, according to one account, "swept down upon the country" for two weeks in February and March. The storm produced 3 to 4 feet (0.9 to 1.2 meters) of snow. **Snowdrifts** up to

A period woodblock print shows New England colonists struggling through deep snowdrifts during the Great Snow of 1717.

25 feet (7.6 meters) deep buried farmhouses and barns. In some places, people could leave their houses only through second-floor windows.

Unable to get through the snowdrifts to collect wood, some elderly people burned their furniture to keep warm. Food supplies ran low. Some villages sent boys with sleds to nearby farms to buy butter, eggs, and milk. Many cattle and sheep froze to death or were buried in snowdrifts. In the spring, their bodies were found frozen solid in their tracks. Hungry wolves, foxes, and bears, unable to get food in the deep snow, came out of the forests to raid farmyards.

A gray wolf stands in a snow storm. During the Great Snow of 1717, hungry wolves raided farmyards for food.

LOST IN THE STORM

One person who experienced the Great Snow of 1717 described the difficulties encountered while searching for people following the blizzard:

"It was not an uncommon thing, just after the storm, for searching parties to go hunting for neighbors, lose their bearings and not be able to locate the houses. Or perhaps a little smoke, curling upward through a hole in the snow, would show where the chimney was. Such was the depth of the snow where drifts were great."

BLIZZARD WINDS

High winds are the main feature that distinguishes a blizzard from other kinds of snowstorms. The weight and force of the blowing snow strengthens the destructive power of these fierce winds.

What is wind?

Wind is air moving across the surface of Earth. The uneven heating of Earth and its **atmosphere** by the sun causes wind. As air warms, it expands and rises. Cooler air then flows in to replace the heated air. This movement produces wind patterns, which are known as **prevailing winds.** Wind direction is described by the direction from which the wind is blowing, so an easterly wind moves from east to west.

Winds from the poles

The **polar** easterlies are cold winds that blow from the **Arctic** or **Antarctic.** Westerly winds are mild and moist breezes that blow across **temperate** regions. When warm air meets denser, heavier cold polar air, it is pushed upward. As the warm air rises, its temperature falls and clouds develop. Droplets of **water vapor** may form ice crystals, which fall as snowflakes. The polar easterlies are the chief engines of blizzard conditions in North America.

Snow covers the entire northeastern United States in this satellite image taken on Jan. 24, 2005, after one of the worst blizzards in recent history.

Driven snow

As blizzard winds whip up the snow, **visibility** drops dramatically. The whirling snowflakes turn the world into a blur of white, as sky and ground seem to merge and landmarks disappear. This effect is called a **whiteout.** The term can also be used to describe the conditions after a blizzard when everything is covered in snow. During a whiteout, people can lose their ability to judge direction or distance and easily become lost. Snow also muffles sound, adding to the sense of confusion.

Drifting

The high-speed winds of a blizzard create deep **snowdrifts** wherever they are blocked by a building or other object. In the blizzard of 1977, winds in Buffalo, New York, and southern Ontario, Canada, created snowdrifts up to 40 feet (12 meters) high. Such immense drifts can bury cars, trap livestock, and make walking impossible. At first, snowdrifts may consist of light, powdery snow. But snowdrifts may become **compacted** as they harden during a prolonged cold spell. They may also become encrusted with ice if they partially melt and then refreeze.

WINDS THAT BRING BLIZZARDS

In different countries, the prevailing winds associated with blizzards and storms often have a name. In the northern and eastern United States, it is the famous Nor'easter that delivers blizzards. In Russia, the northeast wind that sends people indoors is called the buran. The wind that powers blizzards in Siberia is called the purga.

Abandoned vehicles stand amid heavy snowdrifts on an interstate highway near Lafayette, Indiana, after a blizzard in 1977.

BLIZZARDS OF 1888

In 1888, the United States was struck by two devastating blizzards. The first storm, which blasted the **Great Plains** in January, is often called "The Schoolchildren's Blizzard" because many of its victims were children trying to make their way home after school. The second storm battered the East Coast in March. Its winds were so fierce and its destruction so enormous that it became known as "The Great White Hurricane."

The Schoolchildren's Blizzard

The morning of Jan. 12, 1888, was unusually warm for mid-winter on the Great Plains. Temperatures hovered in the mid-70's °F (mid-20's °C) over a huge area that included Montana, the Dakotas, Minnesota, Colorado, and Nebraska. Dressed lightly for the balmy weather, children headed for their one-room schoolhouses, which were often miles from their homes. Farmers ventured into pastures to tend to their livestock or into town for supplies. But just before noon, winds raging at more than 50 miles (80 kilometers) per hour slammed the region. Within hours, temperatures had plummeted to -35 °F (-37 °C) in some places, and heavy snow had begun to fall. Whipped to a frenzy by the winds, the snow assaulted everything in its path.

Survivors of the 1888 Schoolchildren's Blizzard pose in 1940 for a photo in front of their old schoolhouse 15 miles (24 kilometers) southeast of Lincoln, Nebraska.

Caught in the storm

The blizzard claimed at least 235 lives. An estimated 100 victims were children caught by the howling winds and frigid temperatures while trying to get home. Some teachers and their pupils spent a frightening night huddled around wood or coal stoves in their schoolhouses, while the storm blasted through gaps in the walls. Some teachers tried to lead their pupils to safety through the **whiteout.** In Great Plains, South Dakota, teachers tied a rope between the schoolhouse and a nearby building for the children to cling to as they escaped. In Plainfield, Nebraska, teacher Loie Royce braved the storm after running out of fuel for the stove. Three of her pupils died while walking just 82 yards (75 meters). Royce survived but lost both feet to **frostbite.**

"The Song of the Great Blizzard" sets to music the story of Minnie Freeman, "Nebraska's Fearless Maid," who saved the lives of her students during the blizzard of 1888.

HEROINE OF THE STORM

One of the most famous incidents of the Schoolchildren's Blizzard involved a teacher named Minnie Freeman. After the winds tore the roof off her schoolhouse, Freeman saved all of her students by leading them to a farmhouse about half a mile (0.8 kilometers) away. A marker near Ord, Nebraska, commemorates Freeman's actions as a symbol of the "many acts of heroism ... performed by parents, teachers, and the children themselves" during the blizzard.

Minnie Freeman later described the storm as "a blizzard so fierce and cruel and death-dealing that residents ... cannot speak of it even now without an involuntary shudder." The storm, she wrote, "indicated most impressively the measure of danger and trial that must be endured by the country school teacher in the isolated places on the frontier."

The Great White Hurricane

The Great White Hurricane of March 1888 became legendary for its ferocious attack on an area ranging from Chesapeake Bay to Maine and Canada's Atlantic provinces. But the storm also prompted public officials to develop more efficient ways of clearing snow from city streets and of protecting transportation and communication systems from difficult weather.

From fair to foul

On Saturday, March 10, weather officials in New York City predicted that conditions on Sunday would be "cloudy, followed by light rain and clearing." Instead, a cold air mass sweeping south from Canada crashed into a warm air mass flowing north along the East Coast. By Sunday night, torrential rains had turned to blinding snow as temperatures plummeted and winds began to howl. The storm hit so suddenly that trains filled with passengers were stranded on railroad tracks. During two days of nonstop fury, the storm dumped 40 inches (101 centimeters) of snow on New York and New Jersey and 50 inches (127 centimeters) on Connecticut and Massachusetts. The region also suffered about $20 million in property damage from fires that burned unchecked because of snowbound firefighters. The storm's toll included at least 400 fatalities—including 200 in New York City alone and at least 100 seamen on about 200 ships grounded or sunk by the hurricane-strength winds. A former U.S. senator, Roscoe Conkling, was among the storm's many victims. When a cabman demanded $50 to drive Conkling

Snowdrifts fill the streets of New York City after the Great Blizzard of 1888. The weight of the snow caused many overhead telegraph and telephone lines to snap and fall.

home from his office, the eminent lawyer refused, made his way home on foot, and soon died from his exertions.

"Cut off from the continent"

In New York City, people struggling through the blizzard were knocked over and pinned down by the winds. Some were buried alive by the rapidly accumulating snow. Soon, **snowdrifts** up to 50 feet (15 meters) high blocked streets and sidewalks and buried abandoned trolleys, carriages, wagons, and even sections of the city's elevated train tracks. Telegraph and telephone wires snapped and fell. With transportation and communication systems paralyzed, New York City was "as much cut off from the continent as if it had been towed out into the middle of the Atlantic Ocean," one magazine article of the time reported.

Lessons from the storm

After the storm, telephone companies began installing lines below ground to protect them from wind and heavy snowfalls. City officials also realized that they needed to start clearing streets as soon as a storm began, instead of waiting until afterward. In addition, they became more enthusiastic about underground railroads, first built in London in 1863. Boston opened the first U.S. subway in 1897. The first sections of New York City's subway opened in 1904.

ROUNDABOUT COMMUNICATION

During the storm, telegrams passing between New York City and Boston "were actually sent by way of the Atlantic cable and England, crossing twice under the ocean and traversing some 6,000 miles (9,660 kilometers) to reach places less than 250 miles (402 kilometers) apart," a magazine later reported.

Workers in New York City clear the street underneath an elevated train line after the blizzard of 1888 dropped 40 inches (101 centimeters) of snow in two days.

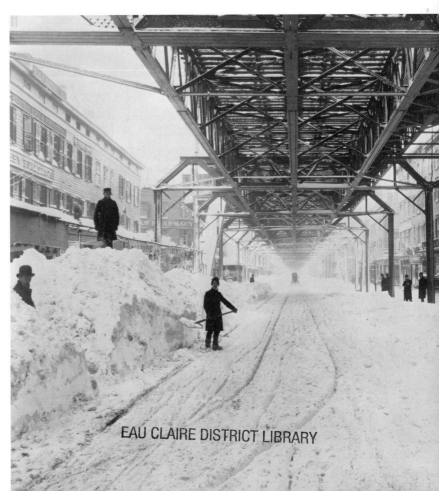

EAU CLAIRE DISTRICT LIBRARY

BLIZZARDS AND THE HUMAN BODY

A hat and scarf provide some protection from the severe wind chill during a blizzard in Washington, D.C., in January 2000.

For a healthy person wearing warm clothing, going out into the snow to hike or ski or for other winter activities can be fun. However, a blizzard can push the human body to its physical limits.

Wind chill

Wind cools the human body faster and to a greater extent than air that is not moving. This means that a person standing outside when the air temperature is just below freezing—32 °F (0 °C)—will lose heat faster if a wind is blowing than on a still day. The measure of how air cools the body when the wind blows is called **wind chill.** People also refer to this scale as the *wind chill index.* For example, if the air temperature is 10 °F (-12 °C) and the wind is blowing at 10 miles (16 kilometers) per hour, the wind chill is -4 °F (-20 °C). Under these conditions, exposed skin will lose heat at the same rate as it would if the temperature was -4 °F and the air was motionless.

Hypothermia

If the human body is exposed to cold for a long period, the body's internal temperature may fall to dangerous levels, a condition known as

hypothermia. If a person's internal temperature falls below 95 °F (35 °C), he or she may become confused or drowsy. At a temperature below 90 °F (32 °C), the victim may lose consciousness. If internal temperature falls below 80 °F (27 °C), the heart may fail. Victims of hypothermia need to receive immediate medical attention.

Frostbite

Frostbite is a major hazard in a blizzard. This condition develops when ice crystals form in human body tissues, preventing the free flow of blood through the vessels in these tissues. Frostbite most commonly affects the ears, nose, chin, fingers, and toes. The affected part turns pale and then becomes a greyish-blue color. A person suffering from frostbite may feel severe pain at first, which then gives way to a loss of feeling. If the blood supply fails completely, the tissue dies, a condition known as **dry gangrene.** Skin exposed to a wind chill of -19 °F (-28 °C) can develop frostbite within just five minutes.

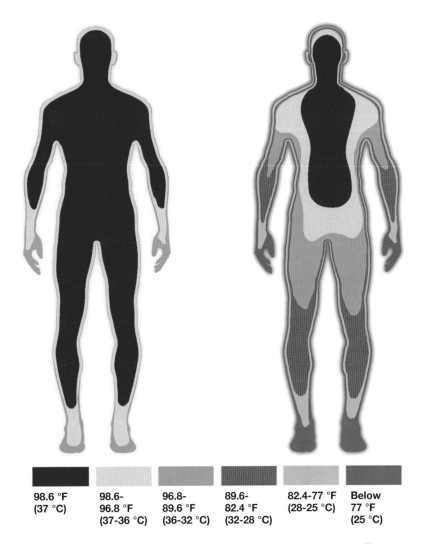

| 98.6 °F (37 °C) | 98.6-96.8 °F (37-36 °C) | 96.8-89.6 °F (36-32 °C) | 89.6-82.4 °F (32-28 °C) | 82.4-77 °F (28-25 °C) | Below 77 °F (25 °C) |

The human body has ways of adjusting to abnormally low temperatures. A normal body temperature is 98.6 °F (37 °C) (left). During hypothermia, when the body is very cold, it diverts heat to the core to try to keep vital organs warm (right).

PRIORITY—SURVIVAL

The human body responds to cold in several ways. In an attempt to rewarm the body, the brain stimulates muscles to contract and relax rapidly, a reaction we know as shivering. The brain also causes blood vessels near the skin and in the hands and feet to narrow. This action shifts blood to the body's core organs—the brain, heart, and lungs—to help keep them warm.

BLIZZARDS AROUND THE WORLD

Throughout Europe, the winter of 2001-2002 was the most severe in nearly 50 years. Heavy snowfalls and frigid temperatures caused hundreds of deaths. Thousands of rural communities were cut off.

Europe 2001-2002

The dreadful cold and snow began in mid-December. On December 13, several countries recorded new lows in temperature. In Switzerland, temperatures at the peak of Jungfrau Mountain in the Alps dropped to -23 °F (-30.7 °C), the lowest in 40 years. During the night of December 23, temperatures in Germany dropped to -50 °F (-45 °C), the coldest since 1870. Massive snowfalls forced as many as 100,000 motorists in southern Germany to spend the night in their cars.

A couple shelter themselves under an umbrella as snow falls around them at the San Marco pier in Venice, Italy, December 2001.

Both freezing weather and record snow continued into January 2002. In Venice, Italy, canals froze over for the first time in 17 years. Athens, Greece, was paralyzed by nearly 4 inches (10 centimeters) of snow on January 5. As tourists shivered at the Parthenon, guards threw snowballs at each other. In the Black Sea ports of Constanta and Mangalia in Romania, wind-whipped waves up to 23 feet (7 meters) high halted shipping. In northern Romania, sleighs replaced ambulances, which were blocked by high **snowdrifts** resulting from wind gusts of up to 50 miles (80 kilometers) per hour. By January 8, nearly 300 people had died in Moscow since the beginning of winter. In the Russian port city of Vladivostok, people fought over seats on public transportation. Army personnel carriers pitched in to help pull buses up the snow-blasted streets.

Japanese blizzards

Some of the strongest blizzards and deepest snowdrifts on record plagued Japan in December 2005 and January 2006. About 100 people died during that period. Many fell victim to accidents while trying to clear heavy snow accumulations from their roofs. Heavy snows up to 13 feet (4 meters) deep isolated hundreds of mountain villages. Officials with Japan's Defense Agency mobilized troops to help clear the snow from roadways and roofs.

One of the most harrowing incidents of the winter occurred on Dec. 24, 2005. Blizzard winds derailed a train traveling across northern Japan, pushing it into snow-covered rice fields along the tracks. The driver reported that after crossing a bridge, he felt the wind lift the train off the tracks. The front car slammed into a building along the line, and three of the remaining five cars fell over. Unfortunately, the storm's fierce winds and heavy snow slowed rescue efforts. At least 4 people died, and 33 people suffered injuries. According to Japanese custom, the president of the rail line apologized to the people killed and injured as well as to their relatives.

In mid-January, rising temperatures and rains prompted government warnings of **avalanches.** Fortunately, the avalanches that occurred caused only minor rail or road blockages in which no one was hurt.

JAPAN'S "SNOW COUNTRY"

The northeastern part of Japan is referred to as Yukiguni (Snow Country) because of its house-burying snowfalls. In 1972, residents in one region, Tsunan, began installing tiny, electric-powered sprinklers in the middle of major thoroughfares. Water pumped from the sprinklers melts the falling snow. Although the roads sometimes become icy-cold rivers, they stay snow-free. And because the water is always moving, it doesn't freeze.

A Japanese man clears snow from the roof of his house after a blizzard in January 2006.

NAPOLEON'S GRAND RETREAT

Winter storms have played a part in great historical events. In the summer of 1812, one of the largest armies ever assembled in Europe marched east to invade Russia under the command of the French Emperor Napoleon Bonaparte. The French troops captured Moscow, Russia's capital. But at the end of October, they were forced to retreat, just as winter set in.

Russian whiteout

From November onward, a series of blizzards battered the retreating French troops as Russian forces relentlessly attacked their rear guard. Starving French soldiers ate their own horses, which forced them to stagger through the snow on foot. Supply wagons were abandoned. On December 5, Napoleon left by sleigh for Paris, but his men had to struggle on.

The retreat by Napoleon's army from Russia during the winter of 1812 is depicted in a period print. Struggling through blizzards and deep snow, thousands of French troops died from starvation, hypothermia, and sheer exhaustion.

The proud army soon became a rabble. On December 6, temperatures reportedly fell to -36 °F (-38 °C). Many soldiers suffered from **frostbite** and **dry gangrene.** Exhausted soldiers collapsed from **hypothermia** and then died where they fell. Some of the French managed to reach the Lithuanian city of Vilnius, where they crawled into monastery hospitals to die. The French commander, Marshal Ney, wrote that: "General Famine and General Winter, rather than Russian bullets, have conquered the Grand [French] Army." Of the 650,000 men who set off for Russia in Napoleon's army, only about 93,000 survived. Napoleon lived to fight another day, but his defeat by the Russian winter marked the beginning of the end for his dream of ruling Europe.

A discovery in Vilnius

Some historians wondered if Napoleon's supporters had exaggerated the stories of the snowy retreat to escape blame for their military failure. However in 2002, a mass grave was discovered at Vilnius. The grave contained the remains of about 2,000 soldiers from Napoleon's Grand Army. Experts who examined the remains learned that many had frozen to death. Others had died of disease and starvation. The experts found that few of the men had died of battle wounds.

OTHER WARS

Blizzards, frostbite, and hypothermia have been common features in many wars from ancient through modern times. In the Korean War (1950-1953), troops fought under blizzard conditions and in bitter temperatures. About 10 percent of all casualties there were related to cold weather.

A group of U.S. Marines take a break in the snow in the intense cold of Korea, during the 1950-1953 war.

THE WHITE HURRICANE OF 1913

Residents of the Great Lakes region of North America are used to autumn storms. In November, such storms are known as *November gales.* The blizzard of November 7 to 12, 1913, was one of the greatest gales to ever strike the Great Lakes.

Creating the gales of November

The blizzard of November 1913 resulted from the collision of two storm systems—**polar** air moving southward from Alberta, Canada, on November 7 and a system of low **atmospheric pressure** traveling eastward across the southern United States. This system had picked up warm, moist air from the Gulf of Mexico. As the winds changed, the system was blown northwestward over the Great Lakes on November 9.

A man watches as a huge wave breaks on the shore of Lake Michigan, by Lincoln Park in Chicago, during the blizzard of 1913.

Ships caught on the lakes

Many ship captains knew that the arctic air would probably cause stormy weather. However, they had no reason to believe that the storm would be any worse than a typical November gale. Many lake freighters, which carried tons of coal, iron ore, and grain between

ports on the lakes and then to the Atlantic Ocean, were out on the lakes when the storms hit. One storm began over western Lake Superior and quickly turned into a blizzard that moved toward Lake Michigan and Lake Huron. At the same time, the southern weather system brought strong winds to Lake Erie. As the storms collided on November 9, four of the Great Lakes were engulfed in blizzards. With wind speeds exceeding 74 miles (119 kilometers) per hour—the minimum speed for a hurricane—the storm came to be called the "White Hurricane." Mountainous waves 35 feet (11 meters) high pounded the ships. The storm raged for 16 hours, much longer than other November gales.

The *Halsted*, a lake freighter, lies beached on Washington Island in Lake Michigan—just 1 of as many as 40 freighters wrecked by the "White Hurricane" blizzard of 1913.

Shipwrecks and death

The storm destroyed as many as 40 ships. Eight large lake freighters sank in Lake Huron, taking all hands with them. At least 235 sailors perished in the storm. For days afterward, residents of southern Ontario in Canada and Michigan in the United States continued to find the frozen bodies of dead sailors on the shores of Lake Huron.

EYEWITNESS

The captain of a freighter carrying coal across Lake Huron from Michigan to Ontario, Canada, survived the 1913 blizzard. However, his ship, the *Howard M. Hanna, Jr.,* sank. Captain Hagen described the night of November 8: "Tremendous seas were coming over our bow ... and over the whole vessel in fact, and the seas had carried away part of our after cabin and had broken in our pilot house window and had torn off the top of the pilot house. ... Shortly before 10 o'clock we could see ... that we were pretty close to Port Austin reef. ... The port side fetched up on the rocks first and the seas and wind pounded her until the vessel went up onto the reef ... and in a very short time she filled with water."

STORM DAMAGE

In general, blizzards cause fewer deaths than hurricanes, floods, and other kinds of natural disasters. Nevertheless, blizzards and other winter storms annually cause about 15 percent of all weather-related deaths in the United States and almost 10 percent of all weather-related injuries, including falls and broken bones.

A motorist gets help moving her car on a North Carolina highway after a blizzard left roads across the state covered in deep snow in January 2000.

Breakdown

In a severe blizzard, people may die from direct exposure to the weather, especially if they are caught outside without shelter or warm clothing. Accidents and breakdowns are also a major cause of deaths during and following blizzard conditions. The high winds and heavy snowfall of a blizzard can knock down power lines, leaving homes without electric power—often needed for heat. **Hypothermia** is a real danger, particularly for the elderly and young children. Power failure and damage to telephone lines can also cause a breakdown in communications, leaving people unable to call for help. Pipes may freeze and burst, leaving homes without a water supply. People without electric power sometimes rely on portable space heaters. But these devices can be dangerous because they can cause fires or give off dangerous fumes if they are used incorrectly.

Transportation systems are often paralyzed during and immediately after a blizzard. Roads and highways may be blocked with snow and **snowdrifts** and abandoned vehicles. Traffic accidents are common and add to traffic snarls. Ambulance and rescue teams often struggle to reach people in need of help, putting lives at risk. Public services may be shut down if employees and officials are unable to get to work.

In rural areas, blizzards may destroy crops and leave people stranded and isolated. Cattle and other livestock out grazing may be stranded or buried in snowdrifts. Many livestock die of starvation before food can be brought in.

Economic costs

The cost of a blizzard is often huge and may affect many aspects of a local economy. It is often difficult to assess the damage caused by a blizzard accurately. For example, following the 1993 "Superstorm" blizzard in the United States, estimates of damage caused by the storm exceeded $6 billion. Estimates may consider only direct damage or insurance claims, or they also may include medical costs and emergency services. The estimates may include calculations of lost business or such canceled services as aircraft flights. If a blizzard shuts down a large airport, taxi companies and other businesses that depend on it will also be affected.

FATAL STATISTICS

■ About 70 percent of deaths caused by ice and snow in the United States are related to automobile accidents.

■ About 25 percent of the deaths are caused by the physical stress of the storm, resulting mainly in heart attacks. The remaining victims are people who were trapped or stranded by a storm.

■ Half of the people who die of exposure to cold in the United States are over 60 years old. About 75 percent are males. About 20 percent die in their homes.

Heart attacks brought on by shoveling heavy snow are a leading cause of death and injury during and after blizzards.

AFTER A BLIZZARD

The immediate dangers of a blizzard are the cold, the force of the wind, and the weight of the snow. However, once a blizzard is over, other hazards may follow, including **avalanches** and flooding.

Avalanches

Avalanches occur when weather conditions cause snow on a mountain slope to become unstable. When a mass of snow breaks free, it slides down the mountain slope, burying everything in its path. Wind gusts may set off an avalanche. Similar conditions may topple a *cornice* (an overhanging mass of **compacted** snow or ice) from a mountain ridge or cliff.

White death

The worst avalanche in U.S. history took place in March 1910 in the Cascade Mountains. A blizzard and avalanches forced a passenger train

An avalanche pours down a gully on Mount McKinley, Alaska. Avalanches occur when large amounts of snow become loose and crash down a mountainside under the force of gravity.

and a mail train traveling westward to Puget Sound to stop near Wellington, Washington. For six days, the trains sat on the tracks. The blizzard ended on March 1 but was quickly followed by rain, thunder, and lightning. The thunder shook loose an avalanche 1,300 feet (400 meters) wide that swept the trains down the slope before burying them under 40 feet (12 meters) of snow, trees, and boulders. At least 96 railroad employees and passengers were killed. According to a survivor, "There was an electric storm raging at the time. ... Lightning flashes were vivid and a tearing wind was howling down the canyon. Suddenly there was a dull roar, and the sleeping men and women felt the passenger coaches lifted and borne along."

Rescue workers search for victims of the March 1910 avalanche that swept two trains off their tracks and buried them under 40 feet (12 meters) of snow.

Freeze and thaw

After a blizzard, deep **snowdrifts** may last for months if cold weather continues. However, if temperatures rise, rapidly melting snow can cause severe flooding as the **meltwater** drains into streams and rivers.

GOLD MINERS DROWNED

The Central Otago region of New Zealand was blasted by a series of severe blizzards between July and September 1863. Many miners, who had come to this region during a "Gold Rush," froze to death in the storms. Additional disasters followed the storms, as melting snow flooded rivers where prospectors were panning for gold. Historians estimate that from 100 to 200 miners were killed in the flooding, but the actual number of deaths was probably higher.

RACE TO THE SOUTH POLE

In 1911, two teams of European explorers raced across **Antarctica,** each determined to be the first to reach the South Pole. One team was British, led by Robert Falcon Scott. The other team was Norwegian, led by Roald Amundsen. Amundsen and his men set off for the pole in four sleds pulled by 52 dogs. Instead of using dogs all the way, Scott took a different route and relied mainly on ponies to pull sleds. Amundsen reached the South Pole before Scott, whose team ran into the full fury of Antarctic blizzards.

The Norwegians set out from the coast of Antarctica for the South Pole in October 1911. The British departed two weeks later from a different location near the coast. Scott's team was hit by the first blizzard in December. The storm raged for five days, forcing the explorers to make camp and halting their progress. When they were finally able to continue, they ran into impassable **snowdrifts.** The ponies became exhausted and had to be shot. Without ponies, the men had to pull the sledges themselves.

Amundsen had a smooth journey by comparison. The route he had chosen was shorter than Scott's and had almost no hills or other barriers. The dogs withstood the hard work and cold well, and the weather was clear.

A member of the five-man Antarctic expedition team led by Roald Amundsen poses with sled dogs during the journey to the South Pole in 1911. The Norwegian team reached the pole on December 14.

To the South Pole

Scott's team was struck by severe blizzards again in January 1912. The men reached the pole on January 17, but they found that Amundsen had already reached it about five weeks earlier, on Dec. 14, 1911. "Great God!" wrote Scott in his diary, "This is an awful place." The Norwegians returned safely to their base camp, but the British embarked on their 800-mile (1,287-kilometer) journey back to the coast in low spirits.

Death in the snow

The weather worsened, and Scott and his men struggled with exhaustion and **frostbite.** On the return route, another blizzard swept in. One member of the team, Edgar Evans fell into a huge crack in the ice. He survived the fall but died on Feb. 17, 1912. The weather grew worse. On March 16, Lawrence Oates, one of the crew, left his tent and walked out into a blizzard to die. His body was never found. The bodies of Scott and two members of his team, along with records and diaries the men had kept, were found at their last camp site. The site was just 11 miles (17 kilometers) from a supply depot where food and other supplies were stored. Scott made his last diary entry on March 29.

All five members of Scott's expedition team to the South Pole—(from left to right) Laurence Oates, H. R. Bowers, Robert Falcon Scott, Edward Wilson, and Edgar Evans—died, victims of severe blizzards in the Antarctic in 1912.

FINAL WORDS

This was Robert Falcon Scott's last diary entry:

March 29

"Had we lived, I should have had a tale to tell of the hardihood, endurance, and courage of my companions which would have stirred the heart of every Englishman. These rough notes and our dead bodies must tell the tale. ..."

HARD LESSONS OF 1922

In 1922, a fearsome blizzard swept up the East Coast of the United States. Just as the Great Blizzard of 1888 forced city planners to develop transportation systems that could operate despite harsh weather conditions, the 1922 blizzard offered a stark warning for architects and engineers.

The blizzard began with a moisture-laden storm system sweeping northward from the Southern States into masses of colder air hovering above the Northeast. By January 28, Washington, D.C., had been buried by heavy snow. Soon, Baltimore, Philadelphia, and eventually New York City were struggling with high winds, heavy snowfalls, and massive **snowdrifts** that brought all activity to a halt.

The Knickerbocker disaster

The Knickerbocker Theater, a new movie house, opened in Washington, D.C., in 1922. When the blizzard hit the city, huge amounts of snow accumulated on the flat roof of the building. The roof collapsed, and the ceiling inside split open. Tragically, the theater was full of people watching a movie as the brick walls, metal, plaster, and a concrete balcony came crashing down, burying the audience. Hundreds of police, firefighters, and rescue workers rushed to the scene and began to search for bodies. In all, 98 people were killed, and 133 people were injured.

People help clear the rubble after the collapse of the roof of the Knickerbocker Theater in Washington D.C.

Roofs under stress

In regions where heavy snowfall is common, architects traditionally design buildings to withstand the weight of the snow. A steeply *pitched* (slanted) roof is best suited for snowy conditions because snow can accumulate to a dangerous depth on a flat roof. For example, a traditional mountain house called a *chalet* *(sha LAY)* in the European Alps usually has a broad roof to spread the weight of the snow. The steep pitch of the roof encourages snow to slide off, and a broad overhang protects the area around the chalet.

HOW MUCH WEIGHT?

Snow loading is the downward force exerted on structures by the weight of accumulated snow. The roof of any building is the area subject to the greatest weight, temperature, and moisture extremes of any part of the structure. Another factor affecting a roof's snow-bearing capacity is *roof dead weight,* or the weight of all the roofing materials. A layer of **compacted** snow 3.5 feet (1 meter) thick will exert a pressure of about 40 pounds per square foot (18 kilograms per 0.09 square meter).

Since the Knickerbocker disaster, architects in the United States have improved designs to help buildings withstand blizzards and winter weather. New building materials that are stronger and more durable are used to help prevent roof collapse. However, these modern innovations may also cause problems. For example, improved roof **insulation** helps keeps the interior of a house warm in winter months. But during the heavy snowfall of a blizzard, the material tends to keep the outer surface of the roof colder, preventing rapid snowmelt. This allows heavy snow to sit on the roof longer, to the point where the weight may cause a collapse.

Even with modern building design and construction with stronger materials, roof collapses still occur during blizzards. At Bad Reichenhall, Germany, heavy snow from a blizzard caused the roof of an ice-skating rink to collapse in January 2006, killing 15 people.

Rescue workers and firefighters search for victims under the collapsed roof of an ice-skating rink in Bad Reichenhall, Germany, in 2006.

THE SUPERSTORM OF 1993

A man walks his dog across a normally busy New York City street, deserted of all traffic during the Superstorm of 1993. The titanic storm tore through 26 states and affected an estimated 50 percent of the U.S. population.

From March 12 to 14, 1993, people in the United States and Canada suffered through a winter storm so devastating that it became known as "The Superstorm of 1993" and "The Storm of the Century." The storm tore through 26 states, affecting an estimated 50 percent of the U.S. population. Its toll included at least 318 deaths, including 48 people lost at sea, and more than $6 billion in damages, including at least $100 million spent on snow removal.

Storm path

The storm, which began in the Gulf of Mexico, struck Florida first, creating a storm surge 10 feet (3 meters) high along the state's Gulf Coast and fueling at least 11 tornadoes inland. It intensified as it moved through Georgia—dumping 4 inches (10 centimeters) of snow on Atlanta—and grew even more powerful as it raked the Carolinas. In the mountains along the North Carolina-Tennessee border, up to 60 inches (152 centimeters) of snow trapped more than 200 hikers.

Following a broad path northward, the storm dumped 20 inches (51 centimeters) of snow on Chattanooga, Tennessee; 25 inches (63 centimeters) on Pittsburgh, Pennsylvania; 13 inches (33 centimeters) on Washington, D.C.; and 43 inches (109 centimeters) on Syracuse, New York. After leaving land near Portsmouth, New Hampshire, the storm swept into Canada, bringing high winds and deep snow as well as heavy seas that sank at least one ship. The storm was followed by an outbreak of bitterly cold air that set 70 low-temperature records from the **Great Plains** to the Atlantic Coast on March 14, and another 75 records the following day.

Motorists struggle through high winds and driving snow after abandoning their car near Atlanta, Georgia, during the Superstorm of 1993.

Superstorm extremes

During the storm, winds reached 144 miles (232 kilometers) per hour at Mount Washington, New Hampshire. In Tennessee, Mount LeConte received 56 inches (142 centimeters) of snow. Temperatures dropped to -12 °F (-24 °C) at Burlington, Vermont.

Wreaking havoc

During the storm, all interstate highways north of Atlanta were closed. For the first time, all major airports on the East Coast shut down, grounding about one quarter of all U.S. airline flights. About 3 million people lost electric power, as snow, **sleet,** and high winds downed power lines. Hundreds of roofs collapsed under the weight of the snow. On Long Island, New York, at least 18 homes toppled into the sea.

DEEP SNOW

The National Weather Service estimated that the Superstorm of 1993 buried the eastern United States in 44 million acre-feet (5.4 million hectare-meters) of snow, a volume of water equal to about 40 days' flow on the Mississippi River at New Orleans, Louisiana.

POTOMAC AIR CRASH

Modern society depends on transportation. But modern transportation systems are extremely vulnerable to blizzards. Trucks and cars often fail to start in the freezing conditions. Regular tires are little use in deep snow. Snow tires may help **traction,** but they are useless in high **snowdrifts.** Abandoned vehicles may prevent snowplows from keeping roadways open. Railroad tracks may be blocked by drifts or break in freezing temperatures. At airports, ice and snow must be removed from the wings of airplanes. Blowing snow and snowdrifts can also block runways. Blizzards can shut down air travel completely for days.

A tragic accident in the United States on Jan. 13, 1982, highlighted the dangerous effects of blizzards on air travel. Following a week of bitterly cold weather, Washington National Airport (now Ronald Reagan Washington National Airport) in Arlington, Virginia, was temporarily closed because of a snowstorm. Before long, flights were allowed to continue, though snow and ice remained on the ground.

A helicopter drops a line into the frozen Potomac River in an attempt to rescue survivors of the Air Florida plane crash of Jan. 13, 1982.

De-icing problems

On that day, an Air Florida Boeing 737 passenger jet was being readied for take-off. Airport workers **de-iced** the wings of the plane by spraying them with chemicals, but the ice quickly built up again in the frigid temperatures. Frustrated by long delays, the pilots continued the take-off procedure but failed to switch on the aircraft's own automatic de-icing system.

As a result, their instruments incorrectly indicated that the plane's engines were running normally.

The aircraft remained in the air for just 30 seconds before plowing into the 14th Street Bridge over the Potomac River. The plane careered into traffic, killing 4 drivers, before plunging into the ice-filled river. Only 5 people, out of 79 passengers and crew on the plane, survived the plane's plunge into the icy water.

The rescue

Crowds watched in horror while people tried to throw lines to the survivors struggling in the frozen river. One man, Roger Olian, leapt into the river but soon had to return to shore to save himself. The icy roads were blocked by traffic, heavier than usual as people tried to get home before the blizzard worsened. Rescue boats were hampered by ice on the river. One helicopter managed to reach the scene, flying in the limited **visibility** of the storm. Arland D. Williams, Jr., a passenger on the plane who was now in the water, kept passing a rescue line to others, so they could be pulled to safety first. He helped rescue several people but drowned before he could be rescued himself. The 14th Street Bridge was later renamed in his honor.

MUNICH AIR DISASTER

Another air disaster in blizzard conditions occurred on Feb. 6, 1958. A British charter aircraft carrying the Manchester United soccer team crashed as it attempted to take off at Munich, Germany. The airport runways had not been sufficiently cleared of snow and slush, and the aircraft could not achieve sufficient speed for take-off. Twenty-three of the 43 passengers were killed, including many soccer stars.

Snow falls on the wreckage of a British charter jet that crashed on take-off at Munich, Germany, in 1958, killing 23 people. Snow on the runway kept the plane from achieving the speed needed for take-off.

THE BILLION-DOLLAR BLIZZARD OF 1996

The blizzard of 1996 dumped more snow more quickly on more people than any other winter storm in U.S. history. The storm, which lasted from January 6 to January 8, hammered cities along a path from Washington, D.C., to Boston and as far west as Cincinnati, Ohio. But that storm was only the first round in what became a four-part disaster blamed for causing at least 187 deaths and $3.5 billion in property damage.

The first storm

Snow began falling on Washington, D.C., at about 9 p.m. on Saturday, January 6. By the next afternoon, the snow was from 13 to 20 inches (33 to 51 centimeters) deep. All along the East Coast, the relentless snow set records for one-day or all-time totals. High winds swirling around snow-removal vehicles quickly undid any progress crews made in clearing roadways.

The second storm

Snow blowers shoot snow off a runway at Philadelphia International Airport on Jan. 8, 1996.

Another winter storm, a so-called Alberta Clipper originating in Canada, moved in only hours after the first storm ended. Another 4 to 6 inches (10 to 15 centimeters) of snow blanketed cities struggling to dig out from the first storm. By Tuesday, January 9,

Philadelphia had set two snowfall records—for the city's greatest one-storm total and for 24-hour total. Officials banned all motor traffic on city streets except for emergency vehicles while more than 500 snow-removal vehicles labored to clear major roadways. Mayor Ed Rendell urged residents to clear the snow from side streets and from around fire hydrants.

The third storm

After a two-day respite—which included sunshine in some cities—the third and final storm struck the Northeast on January 12. Moving north along the East Coast, the storm dumped another 5 to 12 inches (13 to 30 centimeters) of **precipitation** on the region's beleaguered cities. In some places, the precipitation fell as **sleet** or rain.

The final blow

On January 18 and 19, residents of the Northeast faced another disaster—flooding caused by warm winds, 62 °F (17 °C) temperatures, and brief but intense rains that fell into the heavy snow pack. Several feet of snow melted in less than 24 hours. Major rivers in the region flooded, forcing at least 200,000 people from their homes. At least 35 deaths were attributed to the flooding, which caused some $1.5 billion in damage.

SHOVELING SNOW

During the blizzard, some people tried to keep up with the snow, repeatedly shoveling walks and driveways. One newspaper account described a New York City doctor who had cleared his office driveway four times but had to do it all over again after city plows pushed the snow from the street into the building's entrance. "They plowed roads for buses that weren't running," he said, exasperated. "I am a physician. It is a job I must go to. People get sick."

A car and a truck negotiate floodwaters beneath a bridge in Philadelphia, Pennsylvania, after rapid snowmelt in January 1996 caused widespread flooding.

SURVIVING A BLIZZARD

A lone figure struggles through a blizzard in Scotland in whiteout conditions.

Whether you live in a large city or on a farm, a combination of common sense and preparedness is key to staying safe during a blizzard. Blizzard warnings and weather forecasts should be taken seriously.

If weather forecasts warn of a blizzard, the best plan of action is to stay indoors and keep warm. People should keep a supply of preserved food, bottled water, flashlights, and batteries as well as a first-aid kit and battery-operated radio on hand in case a blizzard strikes. To stay warm, have an emergency heat source that runs without electric power—a wood stove, a fireplace, or a space heater—and a fuel supply. Make sure that such devices are ventilated properly and that a carbon monoxide detector is installed nearby.

When venturing out

People should go out in a blizzard only to obtain medical care or for other life-saving reasons. Heart attacks triggered by shoveling snow and traffic accidents on slippery roads are among the greatest dangers during a blizzard. People who must go out during a blizzard should dress warmly in a waterproof coat with a hood, nonslip footwear, and warm gloves. **Insulation** is important — several layers of thin clothing are more effective than one thick layer. Leave as little skin as possible exposed to the wind and cold to help reduce the risk of **frostbite** and **hypothermia.** Cover your mouth to protect your lungs. Never go out alone and be sure to let someone know where you are going and when you plan to return. Make sure you have adequate food and that you rest often.

In the car

Avoid driving if a blizzard is forecast. **Whiteout** conditions and drifting snow can make traveling by car extremely dangerous. If you must drive in a blizzard, make sure your automobile is properly equipped and that you have emergency supplies in case you become stranded or lost. If you are stranded in your car during a blizzard, stay with the vehicle. Make sure the exhaust pipe is not blocked with snow to guard against dangerous fumes and run the engine and heater for only about 10 minutes every hour. Tie a colored scarf or other piece of cloth to the antenna so rescuers can spot the vehicle in the snow. Keep a supply of preserved food and bottled water in the car during winter trips. A first-aid kit, blankets, and a snow shovel should be kept in the car's trunk. If you are stranded without water, you should melt snow before swallowing it to avoid becoming chilled.

POLAR WOMEN SURVIVE BLIZZARD

In 2002, three British women, attempting to set a **polar** hiking record, survived a 48-hour blizzard without a tent. Ann Daniels, Caroline Hamilton, and Pom Oliver were hit by the severe storm with wind of more than 58 miles (93 kilometers) per hour just a week into their 750-mile (1,207-kilometer) hike to the North Pole. Unable to erect their tent, they made a shelter using their sleds.

Red Cross workers in upstate New York search for victims in cars buried under snowdrifts up to 40 feet (12 meters) high during the 1977 blizzard.

CHICAGO'S "BIG SNOW" OF 1967

On Jan. 24, 1967, Chicago enjoyed a springlike temperature of 65 °F (18.3 °C). Just two days later, the city was pummeled by one of the worst snowstorms it has ever endured. Sixty people died during the storm, and according to some historians, the blizzard caused more disruption to area businesses and transportation than any other event since the Great Chicago Fire of 1871.

"Accumulations of 4 inches or more"

Weather forecasters expected the snow, which began to fall at 5:02 a.m. on January 26, to be a relatively light 4 inches (10 centimeters). However, by late morning, the snow was accumulating at a rate of 2 inches (6 centimeters) per hour across northeastern Illinois, northern Indiana, southern Michigan, and several other Midwestern States. When the storm ended at 10:10 a.m. on January 27, 23 inches (58 centimeters) of snow had piled up. Fierce winds created **snowdrifts** 6 feet (2 meters) high.

Caught in the storm

By the time Chicago-area residents realized what was happening, most were either at work or at school. Many left early to head home. But as streets became clogged with blowing and drifting snow,

Snowdrifts fill the streets of Chicago on Jan. 28, 1967, after a blizzard brought the city to a standstill under 23 inches (58 centimeters) of snow.

traffic came to a standstill. An estimated 20,000 to 50,000 cars, as well as 1,100 buses, were abandoned on city streets and expressways, hampering efforts by city workers to clear the roads. In the Chicago suburb of Markham, 650 students in 4 schools never made it home at all—they spent the night in their school libraries and gymnasiums when it became clear that the buses would not get through.

People walk along a snow-covered street in Chicago as deep snowdrifts make the sidewalks impassable.

A gift to the children of Florida

Cleaning up the mess was a monumental task—an estimated 75 million tons (68 metric tons) of snow was removed from city streets and parking areas. When workers ran out of room to pile the snow, they began to dump it in the Chicago River. When it became clear that even the river could not handle such an enormous bulk, the snow was loaded into rail cars and transported to Texas and Florida. Workers joked that the snow was a "gift" to Florida children who rarely got to play in the snow.

CLEAN AIR

For a small western suburb, the "Big Snow" of 1967 created a surprisingly positive effect—the cleanest air in years. According to an air pollution monitoring station in River Forest, Illinois, pollution levels after the storm dropped dramatically as the falling snow attracted particles in the air and carried them to the ground. The traffic standstill contributed to cleaning the air.

BLIZZARD RESCUE

Rescuing people who are injured, stranded, or lost during a blizzard may involve police, ambulances and paramedics, tow trucks, fire crews, and even the military. Rescue teams may use helicopters to reach isolated areas. After a blizzard, social services and charities may be called in to provide food and shelter for people caught in the storm.

Search and rescue

Search and rescue (SAR) teams use a variety of methods to locate and rescue survivors in rural areas or national parks. Teams may travel in trucks, helicopters, and even boats to search. Trained dogs are often used to locate people who may be buried in **snowdrifts.** The dogs chosen must be agile and hardy enough to withstand bitter cold. German shepherds, schnauzers, and Labradors are popular breeds with SAR teams.

Rescue technology available today can be very advanced. SAR helicopters may use *thermal imaging cameras,* which locate people through their body heat. People lost in a blizzard have used cellular

A police rescue worker and his dog search for victims of an avalanche in Chamonix, France.

telephones to contact emergency rescue teams. However, severe weather may affect sensitive electronic equipment and signals and so may not function properly in a blizzard. SAR trucks, helicopters, and dog teams usually cannot be dispatched in **whiteout** conditions and so must wait until after the blizzard has passed.

Clearing the snow

Removing snow and snowdrifts from roads is usually a top priority in cities and along major highways following a blizzard so that supplies and emergency services can reach stranded people who need help. Since the 1860's, cities and towns have used snowplows to clear roads. But these often create **compacted** banks of snow along their route, which can block side roads and bury cars.

In many regions, chemicals such as *sodium chloride* (salt) are sprayed to **de-ice** roads during a winter storm. These chemicals work by lowering the freezing point of water, so they melt any ice that they contact. However, the chemicals are less effective in the very cold weather that often follows a blizzard. They also *corrode* (eat away at) metal and asphalt and can also harm the environment.

SAINT BERNARD TO THE RESCUE

The high mountain pass known as the Grand Saint Bernard crosses the Alps between Switzerland and Italy. Today, a road tunnel carries traffic beneath the mountain, but in medieval times many travelers went through the pass on foot, risking fierce blizzards in winter. Saint Bernard of Menthon founded a hospice in the 1000's to provide food and shelter for travelers. By the 1700's the now-famous Saint Bernard dogs were being bred to rescue travelers stranded by blizzards and **avalanches** in the pass.

A snowplow clears snow from city streets during a blizzard in New York City.

FORECASTING BLIZZARDS

Weather forecasts help save lives when a blizzard is on the way. Blizzard warnings help the public prepare for storms. They also help emergency services plan for disasters.

A meteorologist measures the amount of snow that has fallen at a weather station in the Swiss Alps.

Instruments

Meteorologists gather information about the **atmosphere** from land, at sea, in the air, and even from outer space. They use a variety of instruments, including *thermometers,* which measure temperature; *barometers,* which measure **atmospheric pressure;** and *hygrometers,* which measure **humidity.**

Meteorologists measure **precipitation** using a *funnel gauge.* This device consists of a funnel connected to the top of a narrow cylindrical tube. The diameter of the funnel mouth is much larger than the diameter of the tube. Snow or rain falls into the funnel and collects as liquid in the tube. Markings on the side of the tube indicate the amount of precipitation. To estimate snow depth, the amount of water in the gauge is multiplied by a factor of 10 because a typical layer of snow on the ground would melt to form a layer of water about $\frac{1}{10}$ as thick as the snow. A *snowstake gauge* can also be used to measure the depth of fallen snow directly. This device is much like a ruler, usually with markings at every half-inch (1.25 centimeters).

Tracking storms

Meteorologists track severe storms with **Doppler radar,** which can detect changes in wind speed or direction. They also rely on reports of *storm spotters,* people who watch for storms. Ocean buoys record air and sea conditions. Specially equipped aircraft and weather balloons provide data that meteorologists use to determine the temperature and humidity of the air and the speed and direction of winds. Meteorologists use weather satellites to follow storms and to estimate wind speeds. They also use data gathered by satellites to estimate temperature and humidity.

Forecasts and warnings

Meteorologists prepare forecasts from gathered data and *computer models.* A computer model, sometimes called a *numerical weather prediction model,* is a set of mathematical equations processed by computers. The equations *simulate* (represent) how weather systems form and change.

WINTER STORM SCALE

A scale developed by scientists to rank winter storms in the eastern United States was first used during the 2005-2006 winter season. The scale, called the Northeast Snowfall Impact Scale (NESIS), includes five categories: Notable, Significant, Major, Crippling, and Extreme. To determine a storm's NESIS ranking, meteorologists take into account a storm's size, snowfall amounts, and the number of people living in the path of the storm. Since the mid-1950's, only two U.S. storms have been devastating enough to rank as Extreme on the NESIS: the Superstorm of 1993 and the Billion-Dollar Blizzard of 1996.

Meteorologists check equipment before the launch of a weather balloon in northern Sweden.

STUDYING SNOWFLAKES

Blizzards may be furious and dangerous displays of the power of nature, but they can also be astonishingly beautiful. Nothing is more spectacular than a snowflake. The flakes come in a seemingly endless variety of structures and shapes, but they all have something in common. All snowflakes have six sides.

Equipment

- Freezer
- Black cloth or paper
- Magnifying glass

Instructions

1. Find some sheets of black cloth or black paper. Place them in a freezer until they are very cold. During a snowstorm, take the sheets outside and allow snowflakes to fall on them.

2. Quickly, before the snowflakes melt, examine each one carefully with a magnifying glass. How many sides do unbroken flakes have? This number remains the same in all flakes because of the structure of the water molecules and the way they combine.

air current A mass of air moving in the same direction.

altitude A measure of height above Earth's surface or sea level.

Antarctic The region at and around the South Pole.

Arctic The region at and around the North Pole.

atmosphere The layer of gases surrounding Earth.

atmospheric pressure The weight of the air pressing down on Earth's surface.

avalanche A mass of snow and ice that slides down a mountain slope.

compacted Firmly packed together.

de-ice To remove a build-up of ice on vehicles, machinery, or roads.

Doppler radar A radar system whose reflected radio waves are able to determine the speed of moving objects, used in meteorology.

dry gangrene A non-life-threatening form of gangrene in which a gradual loss of blood supply causes tissue to die and drop off. Complete healing usually occurs at the junction between living and dead tissue.

frostbite Injury caused by the freezing of tissue and blood vessels.

global warming The gradual warming of Earth's atmosphere over many years.

Great Plains A vast, dry grassland in North America that includes eastern South Dakota, Nebraska, Kansas, and Oklahoma.

ground blizzard Blizzard conditions caused by snow blown from the ground.

humidity The amount of moisture (water vapor) in the air.

hypothermia Abnormally low body temperature.

insulation Packing or surrounding material that does not conduct heat.

meltwater Water formed by melting ice or snow.

meteorology The scientific study of the atmosphere and weather.

Northern Hemisphere The half of Earth that is north of the equator.

plateau A raised area of relatively flat land in the mountains or on the sea floor.

polar Of or near the North or South Pole.

precipitation Moisture that falls from clouds, such as rain, snow, or hail.

prevailing wind A wind that blows most commonly from a certain direction.

search and rescue (SAR) The operations carried out by rescue teams.

sleet A type of precipitation formed from small grains of ice.

snowdrift A bank of fallen snow that has been piled up and shaped by the wind.

Southern Hemisphere The half of Earth that is south of the equator.

temperate Not very hot and not very cold.

traction The action of drawing or pulling loads along a road.

visibility The degree to which objects may be seen.

water vapor Water in the form of a gas, found in Earth's atmosphere.

whiteout Conditions during or after a blizzard in which it is impossible to distinguish land, landmarks, or sky.

wind chill The combined cooling effect of wind and air temperature on the human body.

BOOKS

Blizzard! The Storm that Changed America, by Jim Murphy, Scholastic Press, 2000.

The Children's Blizzard, by David Laskin, HarperCollins, 2004.

White-Out: Blizzards, by Claire Watts, Raintree, 2004.

WEB SITES

http://wintercenter.homestead.com/photoindex.html

http://www.ussartf.org/blizzards.htm

http://www.weather.com/encyclopedia/winter/blizzard.html

http://nsidc.org/snow/blizzard/index.html

http://www.chipublib.org/004chicago/disasters/snowstorms.html

INDEX